AF605098

A Story About DIRECTIONS

BOOK 2

Learning about prepositions, directions and movement as we read a map.

TTXME.com
Ten Thousand Method

WRITTEN BY
KAIWIN YEUNG

ILLUSTRATED BY
SIJARJAMIL

DIRECTIONS are like paths we follow
to go somewhere.
Up or down, left or right.
Over or under, above or below.
Directions take us
where we need to go.

For free educational material
and more fun stuff
please visit our website

Special thanks to my little boy, Christian 

A Story About Directions
Book 2 - Learning about prepositions,
directions and movement as we read a map.

Designed in Australia. Manufactured in China.

Written by Kaiwin Yeung.
Illustrated by Sijarjamil.

Paperback ISBN - 978-1-922978-04-2
Hardcover ISBN - 978-1-922978-05-9

A catalogue record for this
book is available from the
National Library of Australia

Ask your local library to order a copy, so others can enjoy this book too!

A Story About DIRECTIONS

BOOK 2:
Learning about prepositions, directions and movement as we read a map.

WRITTEN BY
KAIWIN YEUNG

ILLUSTRATED BY
SIJARJAMIL

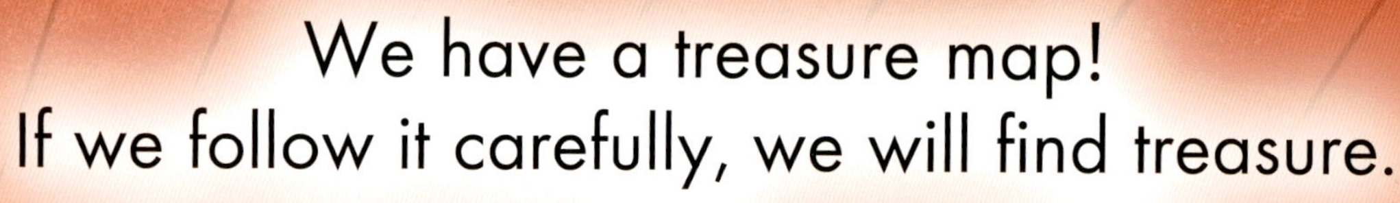
We have a treasure map!
If we follow it carefully, we will find treasure.

I wonder what the treasure will be...

First, we have to start at the bridge.

Go **across** the bridge.

Go **through** the field.

Go **down** the side of the valley.

Go **up** the other side of the valley.

Turn **left** at the fork in the road.

Go **out** of the tunnel.

Go **around** the statue.

Go **under** the waterfall.

Go **into** the cave.

Go **over** the river.

Turn **right** at the windmill.

Go **between** the trees.

Go **away** from the forest.

Go **toward** the harbour.

Zigzag through the stones.

Go **straight** along the cliff.

Go **off** the cliff.

Go **on** to the beach.

Go **behind** the door.

Go **in front** of the portal.

Enter the portal.

Exit the portal.

OUR FAMILY

IS TREASURE

What is your treasure?

Left and right, we search the land,
Up and down, with map in hand.
Toward our goal, we make our way,
To find the treasure we seek today.

The beauty of nature, so vast and grand,
Surrounds us as we cross the land.
And as we travel, our journey ends,
We find our treasure: family and friends.

To be continued...

FREE study material and work sheets at www.TTXME.com

A **map** is a picture that shows us where to find things.
A map of a city can help us find roads, buildings or parks.
A map of the country can help us find rivers, mountains or forests.
And a treasure map can help us find treasure!
A good map will include these features:

Turn to view

The **title** describes what the map includes, and its purpose. The **date** notes the time or period that applies to the map.

Grid lines help us to locate specific points on the map.

The **compass** helps us point the map in the right direction:

North points to the North Pole.
South points to the South Pole.
East points to where the sun rises.
West points to where the sun sets.

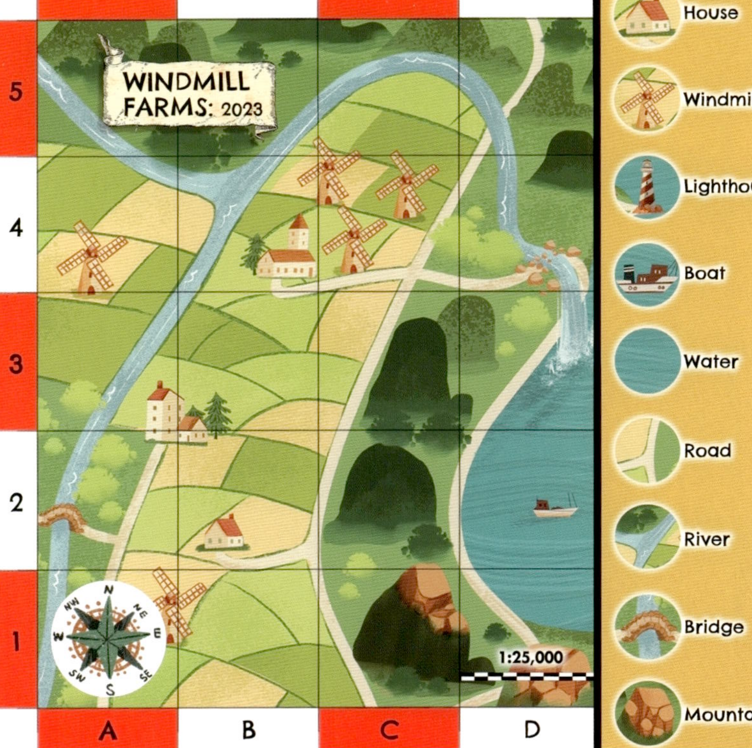

The **legend / key** shows important features (like roads, buildings or rivers) as symbols.

The **scale** is like a ruler that we can use to measure the size of things and the distance between them.

The treasure hunters' map is on the next page.
- Can you find the locations of each page of the story?
- How did they get to the lighthouse, and how did they get home?

LIGHTHOUSE TREASURE
FLOWER FARMS
WINDMILL FARMS
BELMONT RIVER
CHESTERTON
HOME
LITTLE VALLEY
FLOWER FARMS
LAKE SOHO
SAINT HARBOUR
SORRENTO
ANCIENT OWL
EASTERN FOREST
GARNET MOUNTAIN RANGES
Mountain
Bridge
River
Road
Water
Boat
Lighthouse
Windmill
House
N
NE
E
SE
S
SW
W
NW
1:25,000
FREE study material and work sheets at www.TTXME.com
TTXME.com
10
9
8
7
6
5
4
3
2
1
A
B
C
D
E
F
G
H
I
J
K
L
M
N
O

NEW WORDS: **PREPOSITIONS**, DIRECTIONS AND MOVEMENT

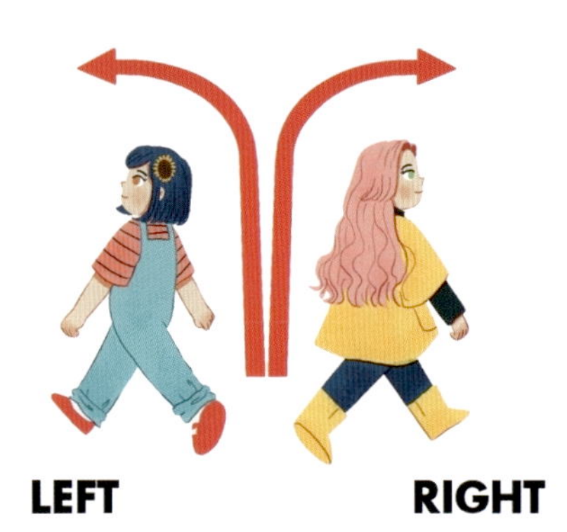

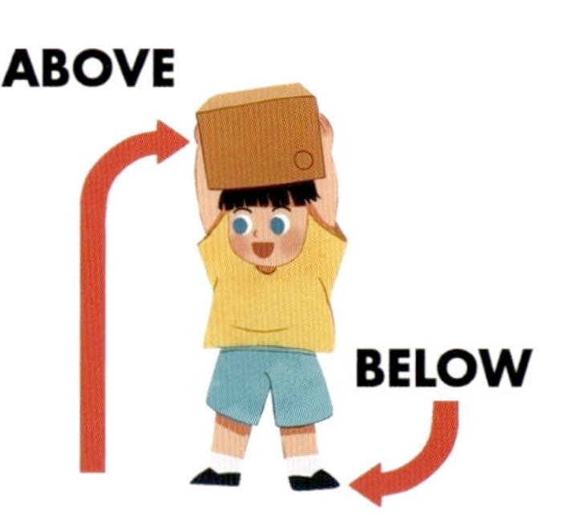

TTXME.com

ONTO
INTO

OUT OF

OFF

IN FRONT
BEHIND

AWAY
TOWARD

BESIDE / AT / BY / NEXT TO

NEAR

FAR

STRAIGHT
ZIGZAG

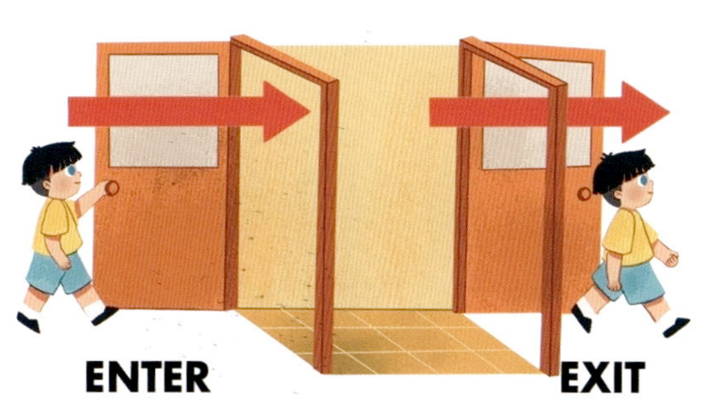
ENTER
EXIT

1st BOOK SERIES
Educational stories
for **early** readers
age 4 - 6.

More books at
www.TTXME.com
Every book contains:

- ✅ fun story lesson
- ✅ warm messages
- ✅ pages of academic resources

Book 4